THE KINGFISHER
First Dinosaur Picture Atlas

Written by David Burnie

Illustrated by Anthony Lewis

KINGFISHER

KINGFISHER

First published 2008 by Kingfisher
an imprint of Macmillan Children's Books
a division of Macmillan Publishers Limited
20 New Wharf Road, London N1 9RR
Basingstoke and Oxford
Associated companies throughout the world
www.panmacmillan.com

ISBN 978-0-7534-1444-6

9 8 7 6 5 4 3 2 1
1TR/0208/SHENS/SC(SC)/128MS/C

A CIP catalogue record for this book is
available from the British Library.

Printed in Taiwan

MAP KEY

~~~~~~~ country border

– – – – state border

· · · · · disputed border

Contents

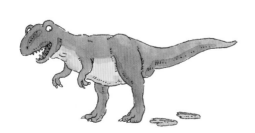

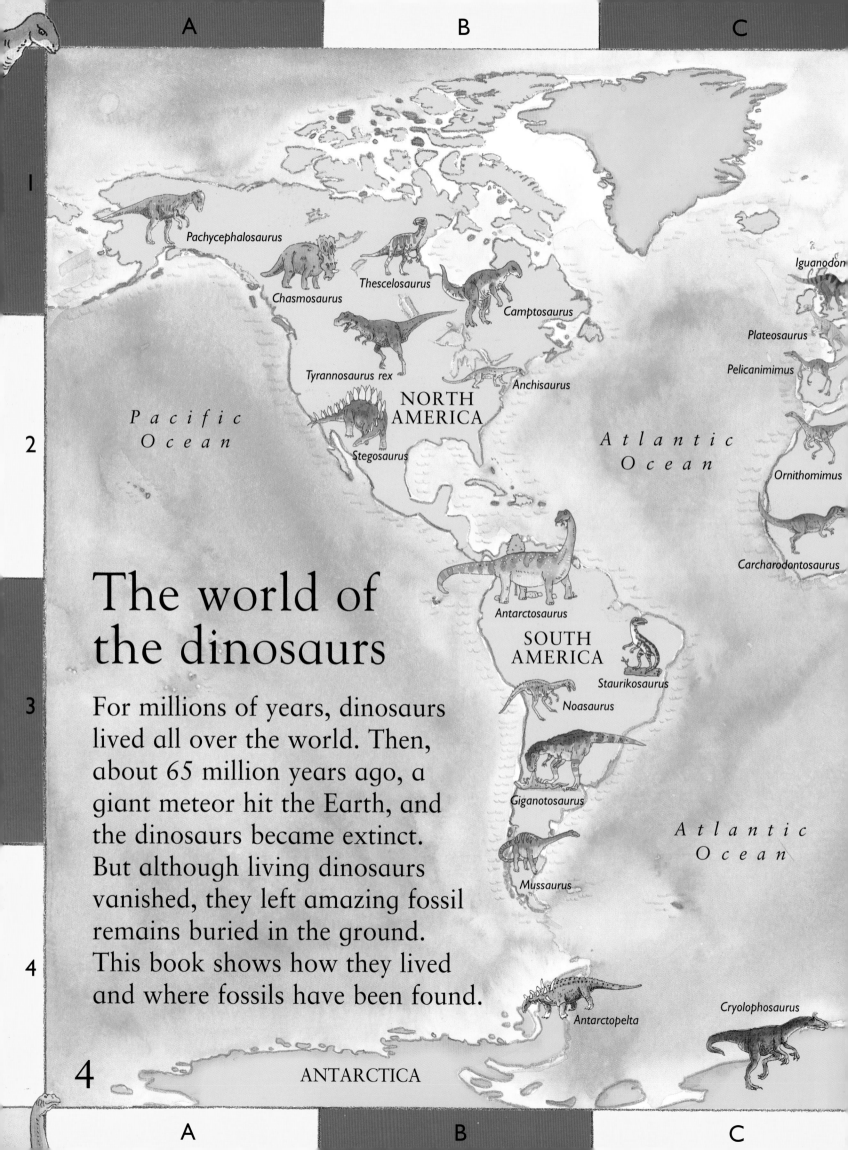

1

Pachycephalosaurus

Chasmosaurus

Thescelosaurus

Camptosaurus

Iguanodon

Tyrannosaurus rex

Anchisaurus

Plateosaurus

Pelicanimimus

Pacific Ocean

NORTH AMERICA

Atlantic Ocean

Ornithomimus

2

Stegosaurus

Carcharodontosaurus

Antarctosaurus

The world of the dinosaurs

SOUTH AMERICA

Staurikosaurus

3

For millions of years, dinosaurs lived all over the world. Then, about 65 million years ago, a giant meteor hit the Earth, and the dinosaurs became extinct. But although living dinosaurs vanished, they left amazing fossil remains buried in the ground. This book shows how they lived and where fossils have been found.

Noasaurus

Giganotosaurus

Atlantic Ocean

Mussaurus

4

Antarctopelta

Cryolophosaurus

4

ANTARCTICA

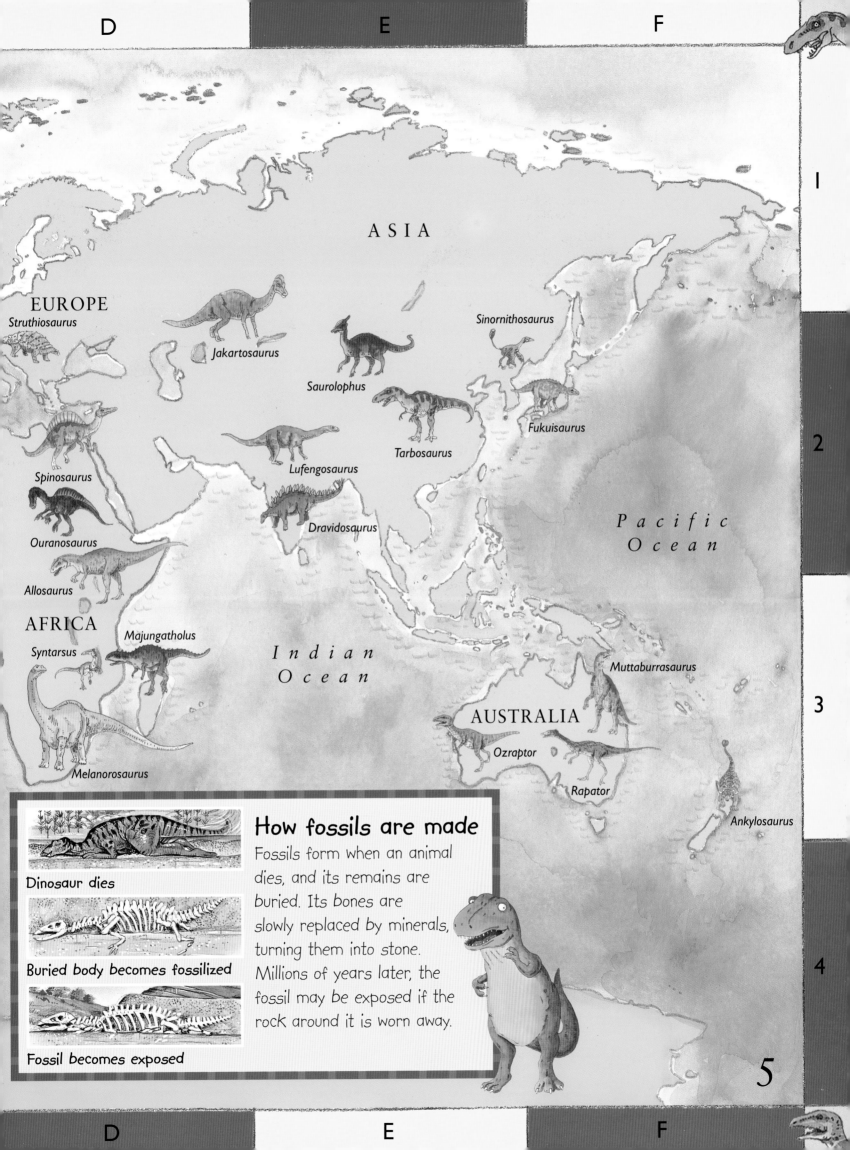

ASIA

EUROPE

Struthiosaurus

Jakartosaurus

Saurolophus

Sinornithosaurus

Spinosaurus

Fukuisaurus

Lufengosaurus

Tarbosaurus

Ouranosaurus

Dravidosaurus

Allosaurus

Pacific Ocean

AFRICA

Majungatholus

Syntarsus

Indian Ocean

Muttaburrasaurus

AUSTRALIA

Melanorosaurus

Ozraptor

Rapator

Ankylosaurus

How fossils are made

Fossils form when an animal dies, and its remains are buried. Its bones are slowly replaced by minerals, turning them into stone. Millions of years later, the fossil may be exposed if the rock around it is worn away.

Dinosaur dies

Buried body becomes fossilized

Fossil becomes exposed

Age of the dinosaurs

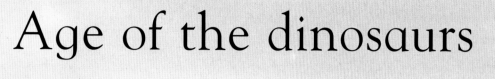

Dinosaurs lived on Earth for over 160 million years. Scientists split this time into three periods – Triassic, Jurassic and Cretaceous. During each period, many different dinosaurs evolved and died out. The Earth's surface also changed, as the continents slowly drifted apart into the seven continents there are today.

Earth in the Cretaceous period

Triassic

Compsognathus

This period started 251 million years ago. At the beginning of the Triassic, most of the world's land was joined in a huge supercontinent, called Pangea.

Dinosaur hunters

The first dinosaur fossils were dug up in Europe, in the 1800s. Since then, dinosaur hunters have found fossils on every continent, including Antarctica. The giant fossil bones being uncovered here in Niger, Africa, are those of a large plant-eater.

Brachiosaurus

Tyrannosaurus rex

Jurassic

This period started about 200 million years ago. In Jurassic times, Pangea began to break apart. The continents drifted apart, taking animals with them.

Cretaceous

This period began 145 million years ago. It ended 65 million years ago, when a huge meteor struck the Earth, wiping out the dinosaurs.

7

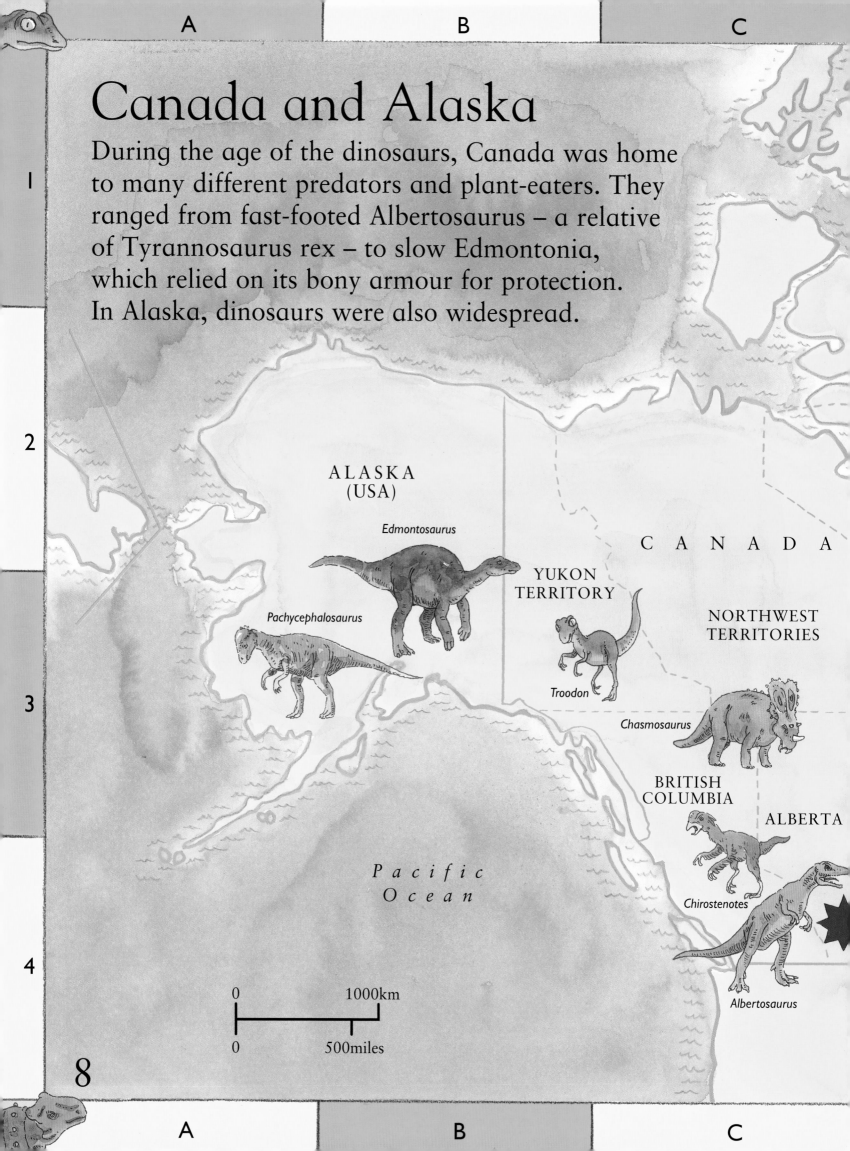

Canada and Alaska

During the age of the dinosaurs, Canada was home to many different predators and plant-eaters. They ranged from fast-footed Albertosaurus – a relative of Tyrannosaurus rex – to slow Edmontonia, which relied on its bony armour for protection. In Alaska, dinosaurs were also widespread.

ALASKA
(USA)

Edmontosaurus

Pachycephalosaurus

C A N A D A

YUKON
TERRITORY

Troodon

NORTHWEST
TERRITORIES

Chasmosaurus

BRITISH
COLUMBIA

ALBERTA

Chirostenotes

P a c i f i c
O c e a n

Albertosaurus

0   1000km

0   500miles

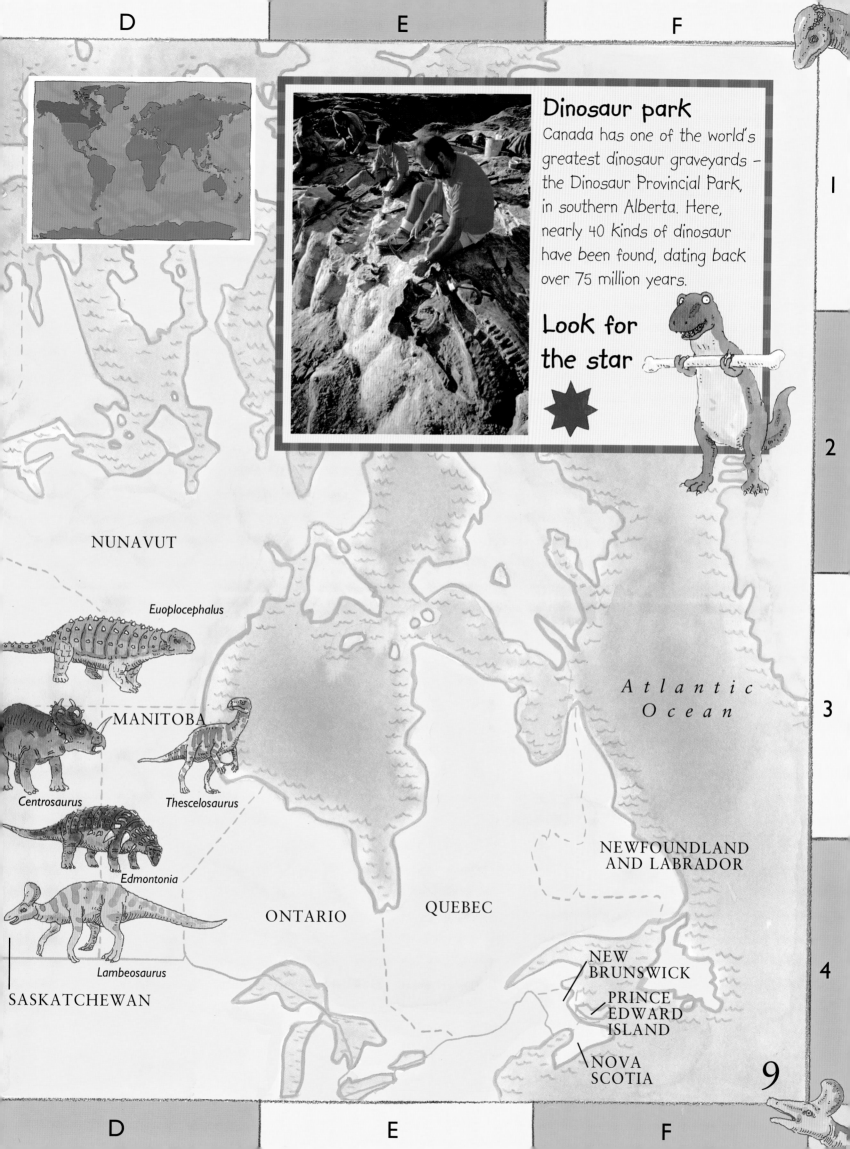

Dinosaur park

Canada has one of the world's greatest dinosaur graveyards – the Dinosaur Provincial Park, in southern Alberta. Here, nearly 40 kinds of dinosaur have been found, dating back over 75 million years.

Look for the star

NUNAVUT

Euoplocephalus

MANITOBA

Centrosaurus

Thescelosaurus

Edmontonia

ONTARIO   QUEBEC

Lambeosaurus

SASKATCHEWAN

Atlantic Ocean

NEWFOUNDLAND AND LABRADOR

NEW BRUNSWICK

PRINCE EDWARD ISLAND

NOVA SCOTIA

Pack attack

In the age of the dinosaurs, Canada was a much warmer place. It was covered by lush plants – a perfect feeding-ground for Lambeosaurus, a duck-bill dinosaur with a large hollow crest. Lambeosaurus had lots of enemies, including dromaeosaurs, which hunted and attacked in packs.

Toothless wonder

Chirostenotes had a bony crest on its head, and beak-shaped jaws without any teeth. It hunted smaller animals, pecking at them just like one of today's birds.

Lambeosaurus

Dromaeosaurus

10

Just for show

Chasmosaurus had a giant frill behind its head. Instead of being solid, the frill had a bony framework covered with skin. It may have been used to frighten off rivals or to attract a mate.

Night shift

Troodon had unusually large eyes, which may have helped it *see* to hunt at night. It probably chased small mammals that came out to feed when other dinosaurs were asleep.

0   1000km

0   500miles

WASHINGTON

Struthiomimus

Deinonychus

Bambiraptor

OREGON

Triceratops

Tyrannosaurus rex

MONTANA

Scutellosaurus

Ornitholestes

WYOMING

IDAHO

Camptosaurus

Parasaurolophus

UTAH

COLORADO

Diplodocus

Gastonia

NEVADA

Allosaurus

Pacific Ocean

CALIFORNIA

NEW MEXICO

Stegosaurus

Dilophosaurus

ARIZONA

The United States of America

Coelophysis

Scutellosaurus

Seismosaurus

America's first complete dinosaur – a Hadrosaurus – was discovered in New Jersey in 1858. But most have been found further west. Dinosaur hunters have unearthed more than 120 kinds of dinosaur, from giant plant-eaters such as Diplodocus, to Tyrannosaurus rex – probably the best-known dinosaur in the world.

Bone bed

The Dinosaur Wall, in Utah, contains hundreds of dinosaur fossils on a ledge of sloping rock. This man is clearing rock around them, leaving the bones as they were found.

Look for the star

I

2

3

4

NORTH DAKOTA

MINNESOTA

Maiasaura

SOUTH DAKOTA

BRASKA

Ceratosaurus

KANSAS

Apatosaurus

OKLAHOMA   ARKANSAS

TEXAS

Stegoceras

LOUISIANA

IOWA

WISCONSIN

MICHIGAN

ILLINOIS

INDIANA

MISSOURI

KENTUCKY

TENNESSEE

MISSISSIPPI

ALABAMA

GEORGIA

FLORIDA

OHIO

PENNSYLVANIA

WEST VIRGINIA

Coelophysis

VERMONT

MAINE

NEW HAMPSHIRE

NEW YORK

MASSACHUSETTS

RHODE ISLAND

Anchisaurus

CONNECTICUT

NEW JERSEY

Hadrosaurus

DELAWARE

MARYLAND

VIRGINIA

NORTH CAROLINA

SOUTH CAROLINA

A t l a n t i c O c e a n

G u l f   o f M e x i c o

13

Dinosaur nest in Montana

In the 1970s, dinosaur hunters made an incredible find in the mountains of Montana. As well as many fossilized dinosaur bones, they found nests, eggs and young. The nests belonged to Maiasaura, or 'good mother lizard'. This plant-eating dinosaur laid up to 40 eggs in a mound-shaped nest, and brought food to its young.

Maiasaura

14

Protoceratops fossil eggs

Dinosaur eggs

Like most reptiles today, most dinosaurs laid eggs. For their size, their eggs were often quite small. Some were round, and others long and narrow. These eggs were laid by **Protoceratops**, a dinosaur that lived in Mongolia.

Growing up

When newly hatched, **Maiasaura** had a tiny skull, and teeth smaller than a two-year-old child's. As it grew, its skull became bigger and longer, giving it a strong bite for crushing plants.

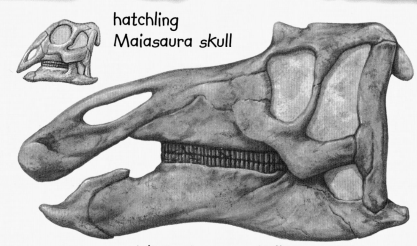

hatchling
Maiasaura skull

adult Maiasaura skull

North American dinosaurs

Triceratops looked fierce, but it was actually a plant-eater. It was up to four times as heavy as a rhinoceros, and its horns could be as much as metre long. It used the horns to fight back against strong predators, such as Tyrannosaurus rex.

Tyrannosaurus rex

Triceratops

King of the dinosaurs

Tyrannosaurus rex was one of the biggest two-legged predators, and lived at the end of the age of the dinosaurs. It ambushed smaller dinosaurs, but also scavenged on dead remains of other dinosaurs.

Tyrannosaurus rex

Scutellosaurus

Danger in numbers

Slim, lightweight and fast-moving, **Deinonychus** hunted in packs. These dinosaurs were able to catch and kill larger dinosaurs that moved too slowly to escape.

Tenontosaurus

Deinonychus

Deadly swing

Ankylosaurus had armoured skin, and a tail club that weighed up to 50 kilograms. By swinging its club, it could smash open the skull of a large predator.

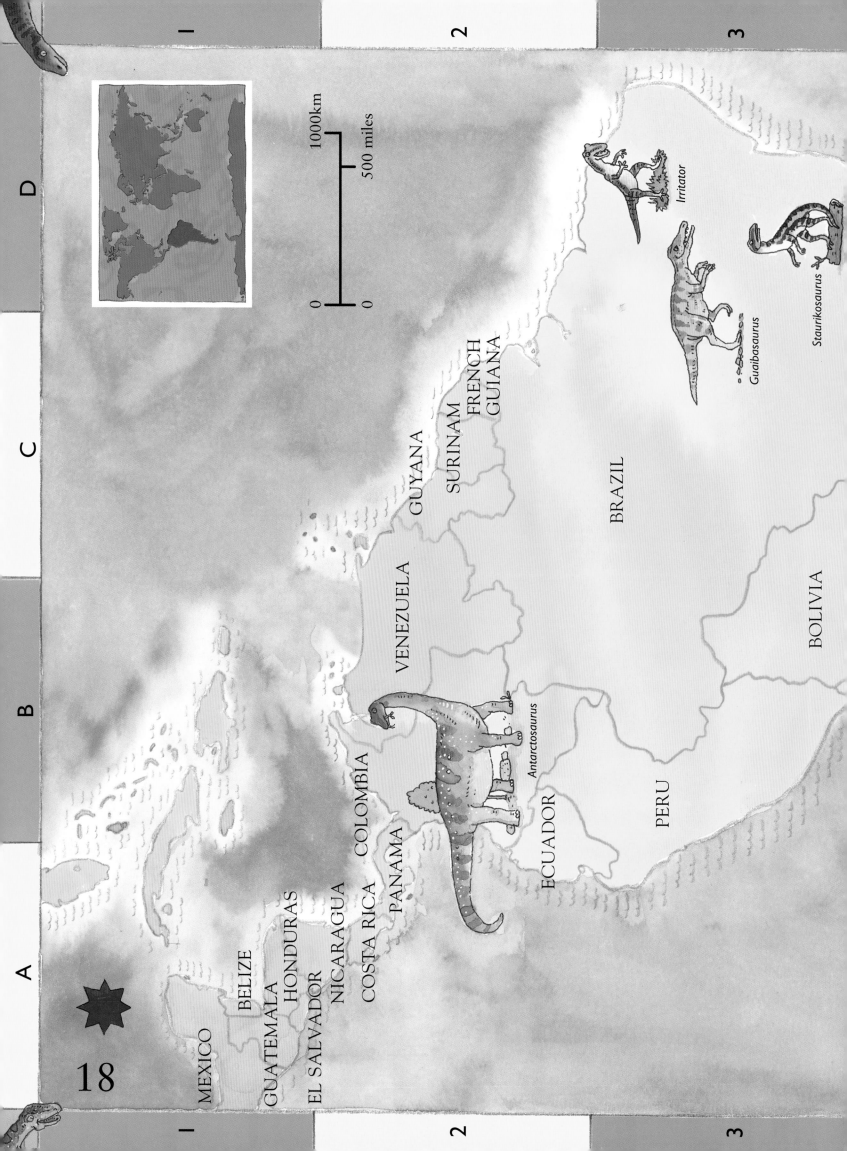

18

MEXICO

BELIZE
GUATEMALA
HONDURAS
EL SALVADOR
NICARAGUA
COSTA RICA
PANAMA
COLOMBIA

VENEZUELA

GUYANA
SURINAM
FRENCH
GUIANA

ECUADOR

PERU

BRAZIL

BOLIVIA

Antarctosaurus

Guaibasaurus

Irritator

Staurikosaurus

1000km

500 miles

0

0

Central and South America

Some of the world's earliest and biggest dinosaurs have been discovered in South America. These include Eoraptor, a chicken-sized dinosaur that lived more than 225 million years ago, and Saltasaurus, a colossal plant-eater that may have weighed nearly 100 tonnes.

URUGUAY

Saltasaurus

PARAGUAY

Herrerasaurus

ARGENTINA

Giganotosaurus

Noasaurus

Eoraptor

Argentinosaurus

Carnotaurus

Abelisaurus

Piatnizkysaurus

Mussaurus

CHILE

The crater is under the sea.

Experts think that the dinosaurs died out after a giant meteor crashed into the Earth 65 million years ago. A huge crater has been found in the sea off Mexico, showing where the meteor might have struck.

Look for the star

Dinosaur hunters in Argentina

In Argentina's Valley of the Moon, scientists have found fossils of some of the very first dinosaurs. One of them, Herrerasaurus, lived 228 million years ago. It was 6 metres long, and hunted by running on its back legs. This kind of body shape allowed other hunting dinosaurs to reach incredible sizes.

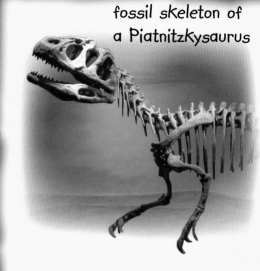

fossil skeleton of a Piatnitzkysaurus

Out of reach

Like many hunting dinosaurs, **Piatnitzkysaurus** had huge back legs but only tiny arms. It also only had three fingers on each of its hands.

Handy work

Eoraptor is another very early dinosaur that lived in the Valley of the Moon. Small and agile, it probably ate small animals as well as plants. It could hold the food it caught with its five-fingered hands.

Going to extremes

Giganotosaurus lived over 100 million years after Herrerasaurus and Eoraptor. It was one of the biggest hunting dinosaurs ever, weighing as much as 7 tonnes.

Herrerasaurus

Eoraptor

21

South American dinosaurs

Carnotaurus was one of the strangest dinosaurs from South America. Its skin was covered with knobbly scales, and it had a small head, with a horn above each eye. It may have used the horns like bulls do when they fight rivals to win the right to mate. The name Carnotaurus means 'meat-eating bull'.

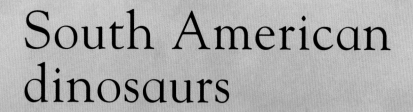

fossil skeleton of a baby Mussaurus

Tiny dino

The smallest complete dinosaur fossil is a baby **Mussaurus,** from Argentina. It measures just 18 centimetres. Mussaurus fed on plants. When fully grown, it probably grew to 5 metres.

Carnotaurus

Tipping the scales

Saltasaurus was a plant-eater that
lived in Argentina. Its back was
covered with hard bony plates, like
those that protect today's crocodiles.

Slashing claw

Noasaurus may have had slashing
claws on its hands. Measuring just
2.5 metres from head to tail, it
would have been light enough to
be able to leap on its prey.

Europe

In Europe, dinosaur fossils have been studied since the early 1800s, when naturalists worked out that they belonged to giant extinct reptiles. Since then, a huge variety of fossils have been found, including giant plant-eaters such as Brachiosaurus, and also Baryonyx – one of the few dinosaurs that fed mainly on fish.

Early bird

Europe's fossils include many other prehistoric animals apart from dinosaurs. The world's earliest known bird, called **Archaeopteryx**, was discovered in a limestone quarry in southern Germany. About the size of a crow, it had teeth and a long bony tail. However, it also had feathers and could fly.

Can you find Archaeopteryx?

fossil skeleton of an Archaeopteryx

North Sea

Saltosaurus

SCOTLAND

UNITED KINGDOM

Megalosaurus

Eustreptospondylus

NORTHERN IRELAND

WALES

ENGLAND

IRELAND

NETHERLANDS

A B C D

1 2 3

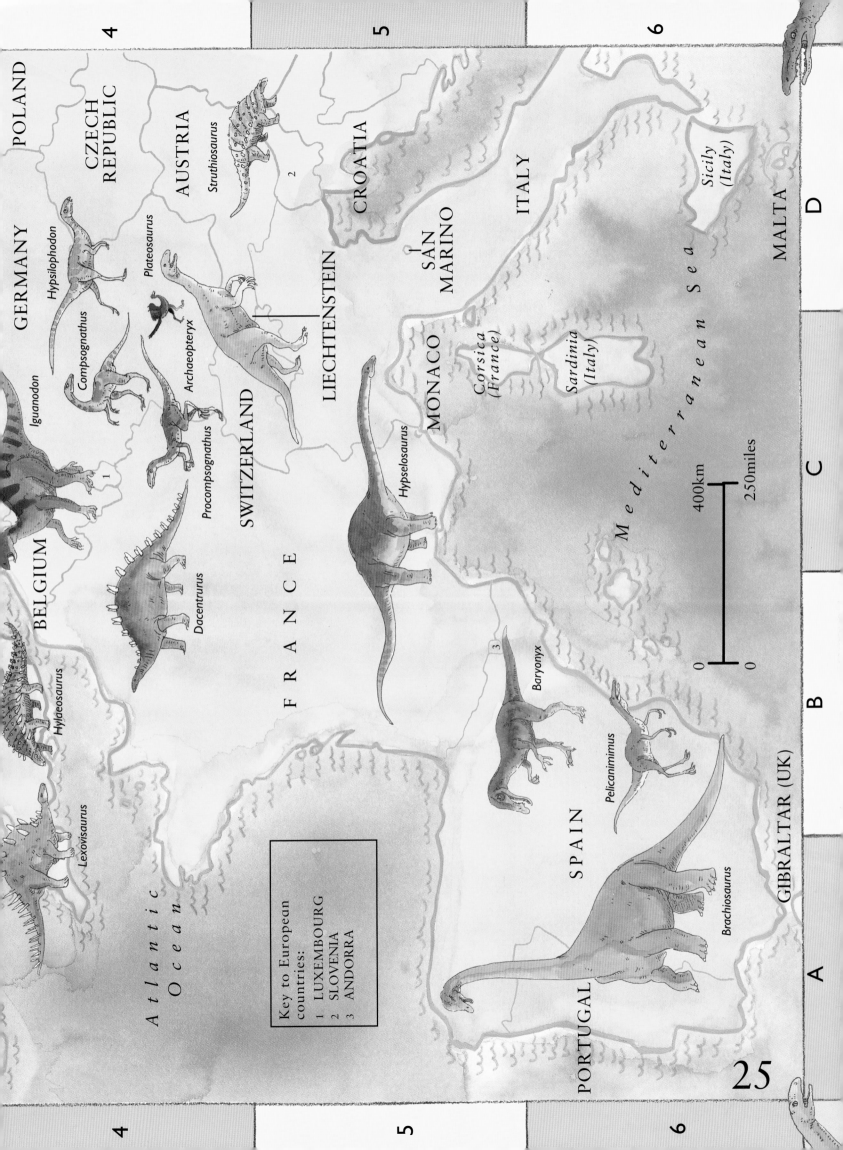

Dinosaur herd in Belgium

In 1878, a team of Belgian miners found 38 Iguanodon skeletons – the remains of a herd that lived over 120 million years ago. The dinosaurs may have died when they tried to escape from predators, and fell into a deep ravine.

fossil Iguanodon skeletons

Fossil herd

The skeletons of the Belgian **Iguanodon** herd are kept together in a museum. It is the largest display of a single kind of dinosaur anywhere in the world.

Iguanodon

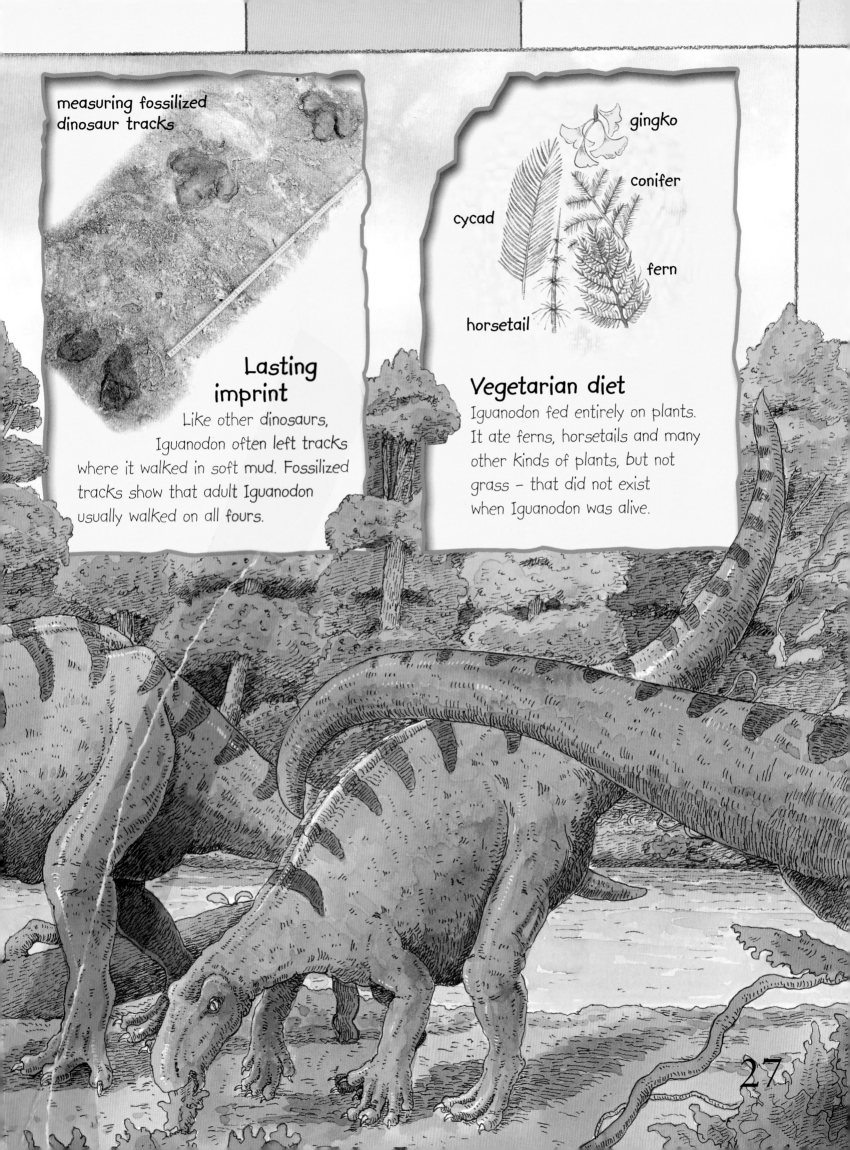

measuring fossilized dinosaur tracks

gingko

conifer

cycad

fern

horsetail

Lasting imprint

Like other dinosaurs, Iguanodon often left tracks where it walked in soft mud. Fossilized tracks show that adult Iguanodon usually walked on all fours.

Vegetarian diet

Iguanodon fed entirely on plants. It ate ferns, horsetails and many other kinds of plants, but not grass – that did not exist when Iguanodon was alive.

27

European dinosaurs

Most dinosaurs fed on land, but Baryonyx was different. It had jaws like a crocodile's, and long claws, particularly on its thumbs. It probably waded into the shallows of rivers and lakes, and caught fish as they swam past. One fossil of Baryonyx from southern England has fish bones and scales inside it.

Baryonyx

Feeding in the treetops

Brachiosaurus was up to 25 metres long, and its crane-like neck could reach nearly twice as high as a giraffe's. It fed on leaves, tearing them off with its peg-shaped teeth. This sauropod lived in Europe, North America and Africa.

Little nipper

One of the smallest plant-eating dinosaurs, **Hypsilophodon** had a head the size of an adult man's hand. It fed on low-growing plants, grinding them up with ridged teeth. It lived in herds, and relied on speed and keen senses to escape danger, just like deer do today.

fossil of a
Hypsilophodon skull

Chasing lizards

Compsognathus was a small, speedy dinosaur, with a chicken-sized body, and a long neck and tail. It fed on lizards and other small animals, tearing them up with its claws and teeth.

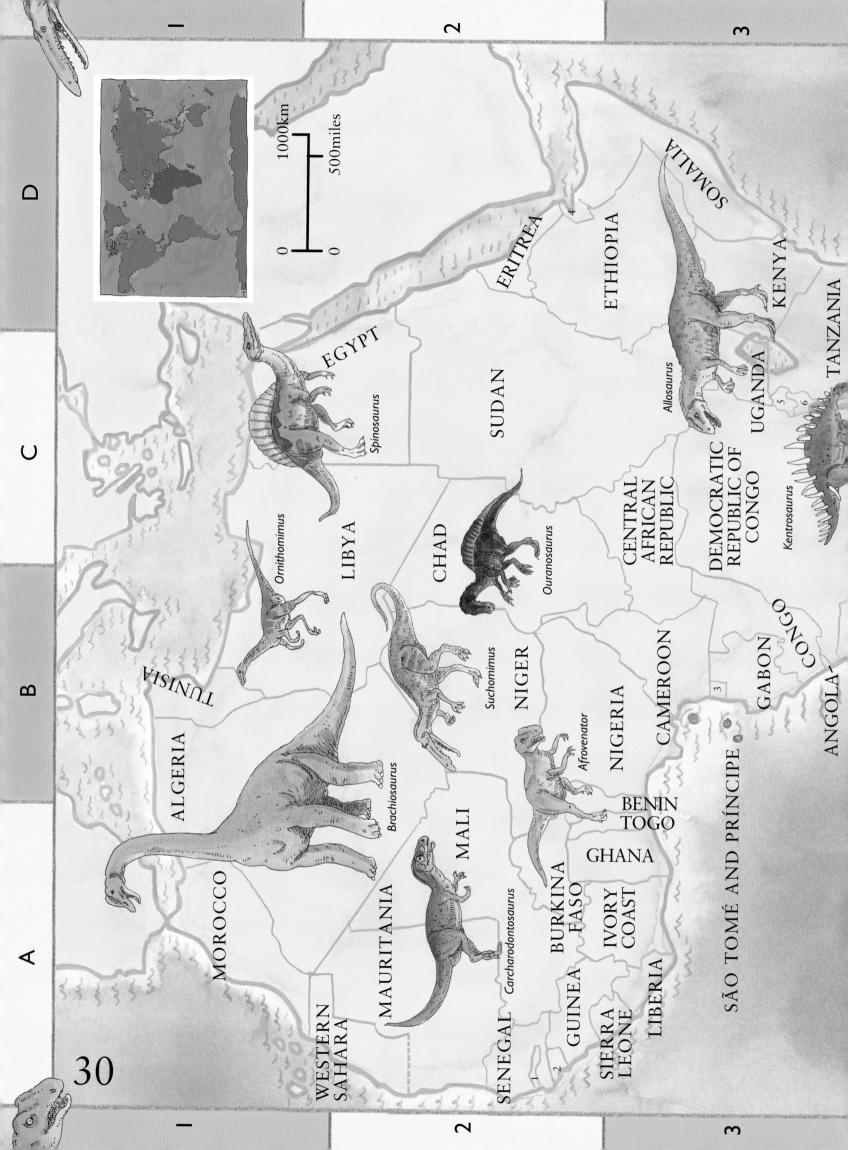

D   C   B   A

1   2   3

MOROCCO

ALGERIA

TUNISIA

LIBYA

EGYPT

WESTERN
SAHARA

MAURITANIA

MALI

NIGER

CHAD

SUDAN

ERITREA

ETHIOPIA

SENEGAL

GUINEA

SIERRA
LEONE

LIBERIA

IVORY
COAST

BURKINA
FASO

GHANA

BENIN
TOGO

NIGERIA

CAMEROON

CENTRAL
AFRICAN
REPUBLIC

DEMOCRATIC
REPUBLIC OF
CONGO

UGANDA

KENYA

SOMALIA

TANZANIA

GABON

CONGO

ANGOLA-

SÃO TOMÉ AND PRÍNCIPE

Spinosaurus

Ornithomimus

Ouranosaurus

Brachiosaurus

Suchomimus

Afrovenator

Carcharodontosaurus

Allosaurus

Kentrosaurus

1000km

500miles

0

0

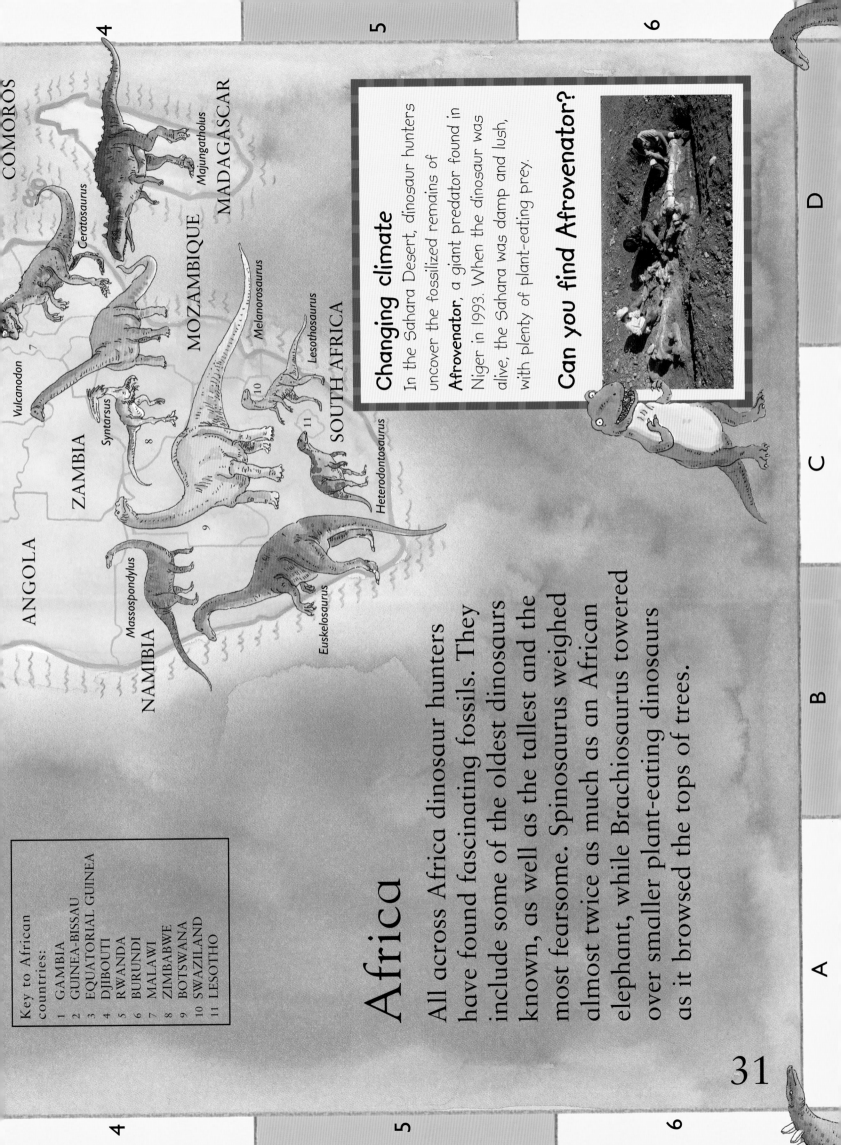

Key to African
countries:
1 GAMBIA
2 GUINEA-BISSAU
3 EQUATORIAL GUINEA
4 DJIBOUTI
5 RWANDA
6 BURUNDI
7 MALAWI
8 ZIMBABWE
9 BOTSWANA
10 SWAZILAND
11 LESOTHO

MADAGASCAR

MOZAMBIQUE

Majungatholus

Ceratosaurus

Vulcanodon

ZAMBIA

Syntarsus

Melanorosaurus

Lesothosaurus

SOUTH AFRICA

Heterodontosaurus

ANGOLA

Massospondylus

NAMIBIA

Euskelosaurus

Changing climate

In the Sahara Desert, dinosaur hunters uncover the fossilized remains of **Afrovenator**, a giant predator found in Niger in 1993. When the dinosaur was alive, the Sahara was damp and lush, with plenty of plant-eating prey.

Can you find Afrovenator?

Africa

All across Africa dinosaur hunters have found fascinating fossils. They include some of the oldest dinosaurs known, as well as the tallest and the most fearsome. Spinosaurus weighed almost twice as much as an African elephant, while Brachiosaurus towered over smaller plant-eating dinosaurs as it browsed the tops of trees.

Duel in Tanzania

In East Africa, a hungry Ceratosaurus tries to attack Kentrosaurus, a slow-moving plant-eater. Kentrosaurus is smaller, but protected by bony plates and spikes up to 60 centimetres long. Each time the predator moves in, Kentrosaurus swivels around and lashes out with its tail.

Ceratosaurus

Kentrosaurus

Big is best

Brachiosaurus relied on sheer size to keep out of danger. This enormous plant-eater may have weighed up to 80 tonnes – vastly more than the biggest predators of its time. But when this giant grew old and weak, it was easy prey to a Ceratosaurus.

Brachiosaurus

Ceratosaurus

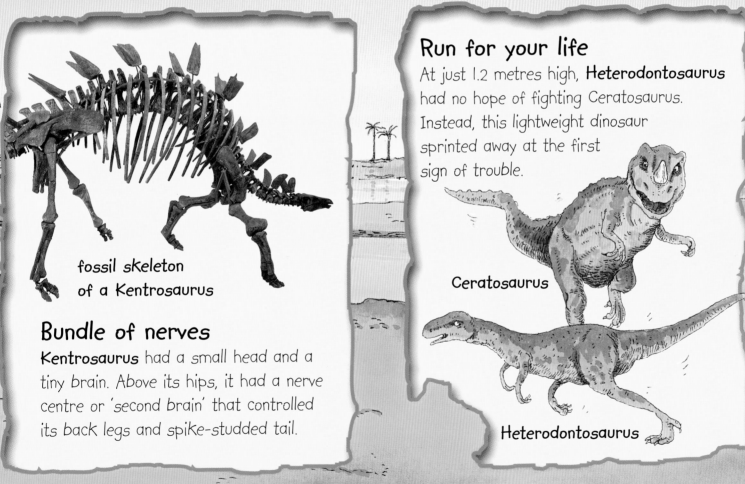

fossil skeleton
of a Kentrosaurus

Run for your life

At just 1.2 metres high, **Heterodontosaurus** had no hope of fighting Ceratosaurus. Instead, this lightweight dinosaur sprinted away at the first sign of trouble.

Ceratosaurus

Heterodontosaurus

Bundle of nerves

Kentrosaurus had a small head and a tiny brain. Above its hips, it had a nerve centre or 'second brain' that controlled its back legs and spike-studded tail.

33

African dinosaurs

Spinosaurus was one of the largest predatory dinosaurs, weighing as much as 9 tonnes. As well as having fearsome teeth and powerful jaws, it had a 2 metre-high 'sail'. It may have used the sail like a solar panel, soaking up warmth at sunrise and sunset.

Spinosaurus

Quick exit

Massopondylus lived about 190 million years ago, towards the beginning of the age of the dinosaurs. It fed mainly on plants, and was lightly built. If danger threatened, it sped away on its back legs.

fossil skull of a Carcharadontosaurus

Giant bite

For sheer biting power, few dinosaurs could match **Carcharadontosaurus**. Its skull was 1.6 metres long. Its teeth had serrated edges, and the biggest were almost as long as a human skull.

Clever hunter

In 1993, researchers found the skeleton of an unknown dinosaur in the Sahara Desert. Although it was 125 million years old, the fossil was almost complete. Called **Afrovenator** – 'African hunter' – it was about 9 metres long. It may have hunted fish in shallow water.

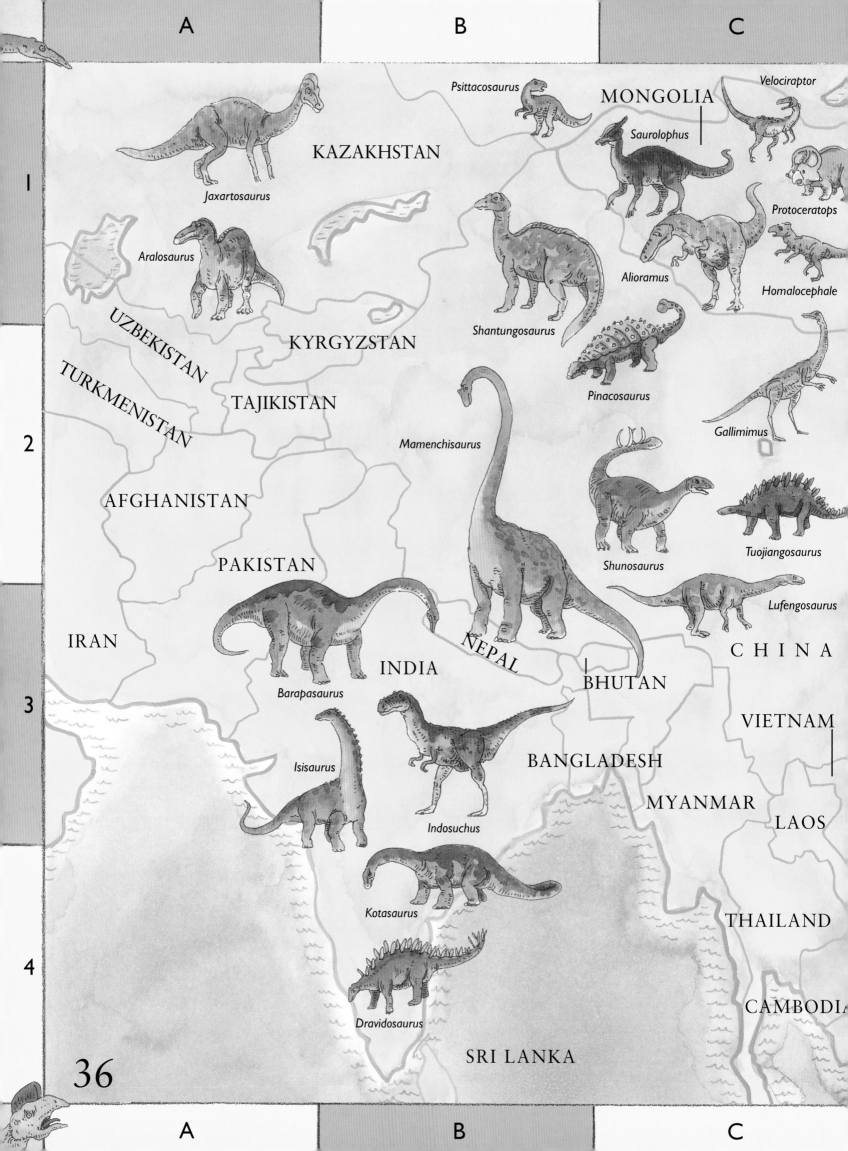

1

2

3

4

Psittacosaurus

MONGOLIA

Velociraptor

Saurolophus

KAZAKHSTAN

Jaxartosaurus

Protoceratops

Aralosaurus

Alioramus

Homalocephale

UZBEKISTAN

KYRGYZSTAN

Shantungosaurus

TURKMENISTAN

TAJIKISTAN

Pinacosaurus

Gallimimus

Mamenchisaurus

AFGHANISTAN

Tuojiangosaurus

Shunosaurus

PAKISTAN

Lufengosaurus

IRAN

NEPAL

C H I N A

Barapasaurus

INDIA

BHUTAN

VIETNAM

Isisaurus

BANGLADESH

Indosuchus

MYANMAR

LAOS

Kotasaurus

THAILAND

CAMBODIA

Dravidosaurus

SRI LANKA

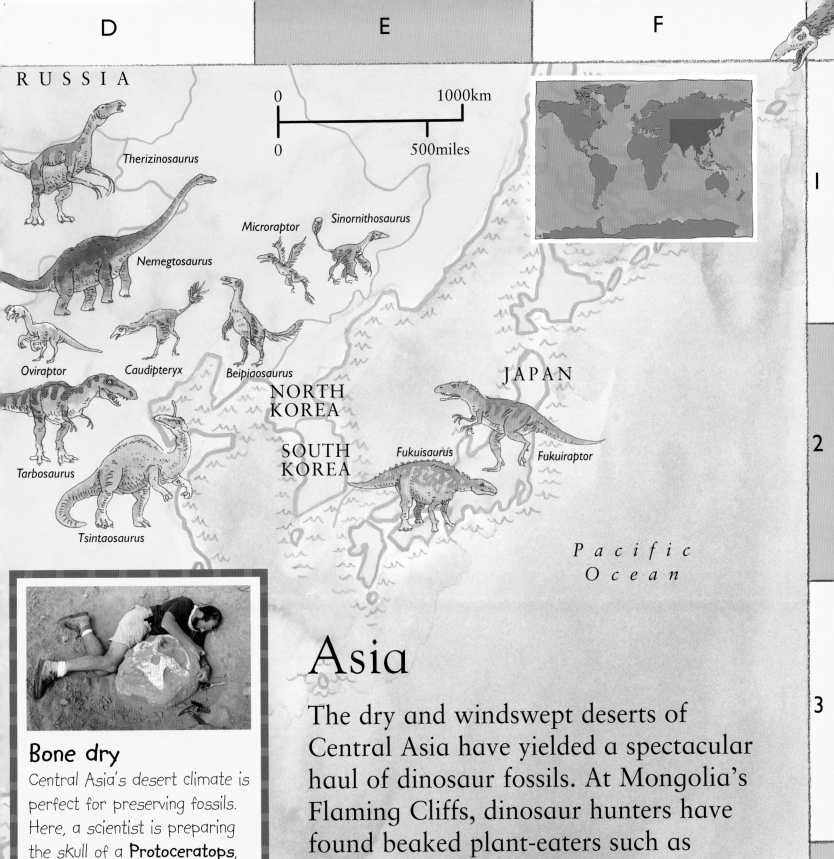

RUSSIA

0 — 1000km

0 — 500miles

Therizinosaurus

Nemegtosaurus

Microraptor

Sinornithosaurus

Oviraptor

Caudipteryx

Beipiaosaurus

NORTH KOREA

SOUTH KOREA

Fukuisaurus

JAPAN

Fukuiraptor

Tarbosaurus

Tsintaosaurus

Pacific Ocean

Bone dry

Central Asia's desert climate is perfect for preserving fossils. Here, a scientist is preparing the skull of a **Protoceratops**, so that it can be removed without breaking apart.

Can you find Protoceratops?

Asia

The dry and windswept deserts of Central Asia have yielded a spectacular haul of dinosaur fossils. At Mongolia's Flaming Cliffs, dinosaur hunters have found beaked plant-eaters such as Protoceratops, fleet-footed hunters such as Velociraptor, and amazing collections of dinosaur eggs. Further east, in China, feathered dinosaurs show how birds evolved flight.

Asian dinosaurs

Most of today's reptiles make no noise, but dinosaurs were very different. Saurolophus, from Asia and North America, made calls by inflating a pouch of skin that was above its snout. These calls would have filled the air when a whole Saurolophus herd spotted danger heading their way.

Large beak
Psittacosaurus, a plant-eater, had a beak like a parrot's. It stood just over one metre high at the shoulder, but reached plants higher up by standing on its back legs.

Tarbosaurus

Saurolophus

Scary claws

In the late 1960s, researchers in Mongolia found a huge pair of arms ending in 25 centimetre-long claws. Very few other bones of their owner, **Deinocheirus,** have been found.

scientist examining Deinocheirus fossil arms

Nest raider

Gallimimus fed on the eggs and young of other dinosaurs, using its arms to dig up and handle food. Its long neck gave it a good view, helping it to spot food at a distance.

Dinosaur fight in Mongolia

Velociraptor and Protoceratops were deadly enemies. One fossil, found in the Gobi desert, shows them locked in combat. Velociraptor was attacking with its claws, while Protoceratops hit back with its beak. They died suddenly, probably because they were smothered by a sand storm, or buried by a collapsing dune.

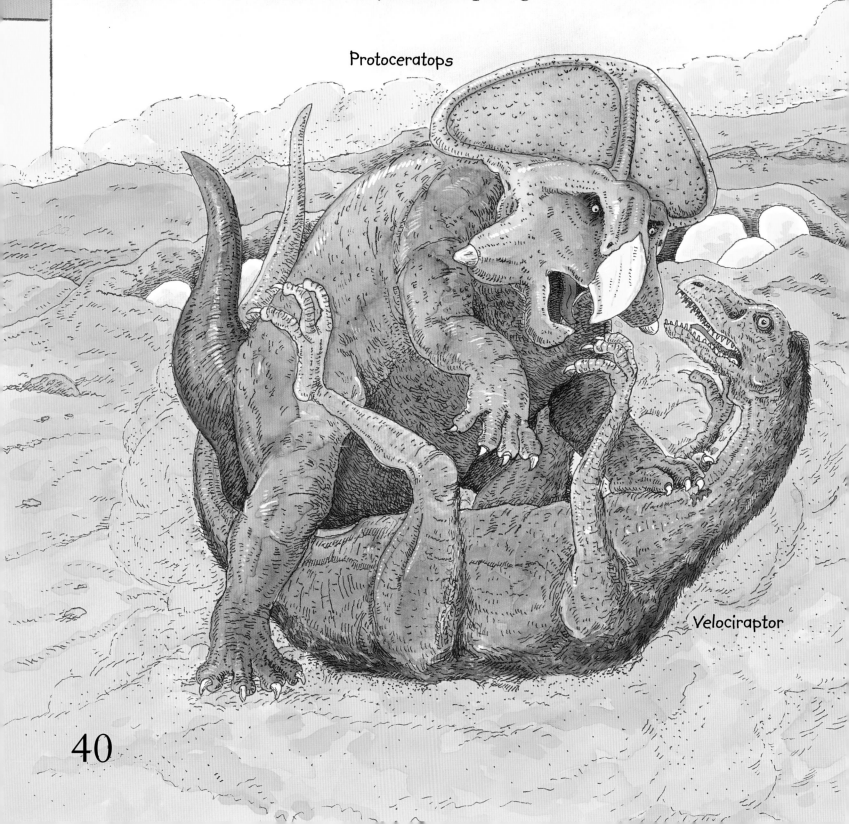

Protoceratops

Velociraptor

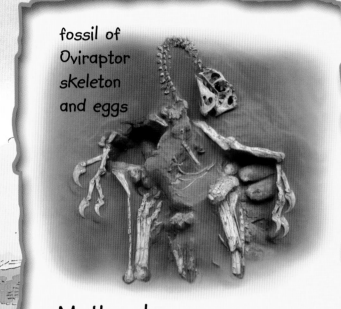
fossil of Oviraptor skeleton and eggs

Mother love

Some dinosaurs were very careful parents. This fossil is of an adult **Oviraptor** that died while sitting on its eggs. Inside each egg, there are the tiny bones of the young.

Low blows

The plant-eater **Pinacosaurus** fought its enemies with a club on the end of its tail. By swinging the club close to the ground, it could smash a predator's legs, knocking them off their feet. Bony armour also helped to keep it out of trouble.

Head-to-head collision

Homalocephale had an extra-thick layer of bone on the top of its skull. The males may have used this in head-butting contests, fighting to attract a mate.

Feathered dinosaurs of China

At Liaoning, in eastern China, researchers have found dinosaurs with fuzzy outlines of feathers instead of scaly skin. Some – including Caudipteryx – used feathers to keep warm. Others had bigger feathers, and used them to fly. Scientists are certain that birds evolved from dinosaurs.

Caudipteryx

pointed scale

fluffy feather

feather with vanes

From scales to feathers

Feathers evolved gradually from hard, pointed scales. Fluffy feathers evolved first, helping to keep dinosaurs warm. From these came much bigger feathers with branched vanes – the kind that were inherited by the world's first true birds.

Ground attack

Protarchaeopteryx had long feathers on its arms, but it could not fly. It probably used its feathers like a scoop, to catch insects and other small animals.

Winged flier

Microraptor was one of the smallest dinosaurs. It had feathers on its legs as well as its arms, and it probably used all four limbs to fly. Instead of taking off from the ground, it may have jumped from trees.

Australia and New Zealand

Not many dinosaurs have been found in Australia.
This is partly because much of Australia was
covered by the sea for much of the age of
the dinosaurs. Even so, Australia was home
to unusual dinosaurs, including the giant
sauropod Austrosaurus, and Minmi,
an armoured dinosaur covered
with bony plates.

Dinosaur trackway

A U S T R A L I A

W E S T E R N
A U S T R A L I A

Dino tracks

Australia has some of the
best preserved dinosaur
trackways. One set,
in Western Australia,
contains giant footprints
over a metre wide.

Can you find
the trackway?

Ozraptor

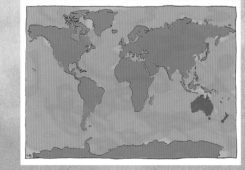

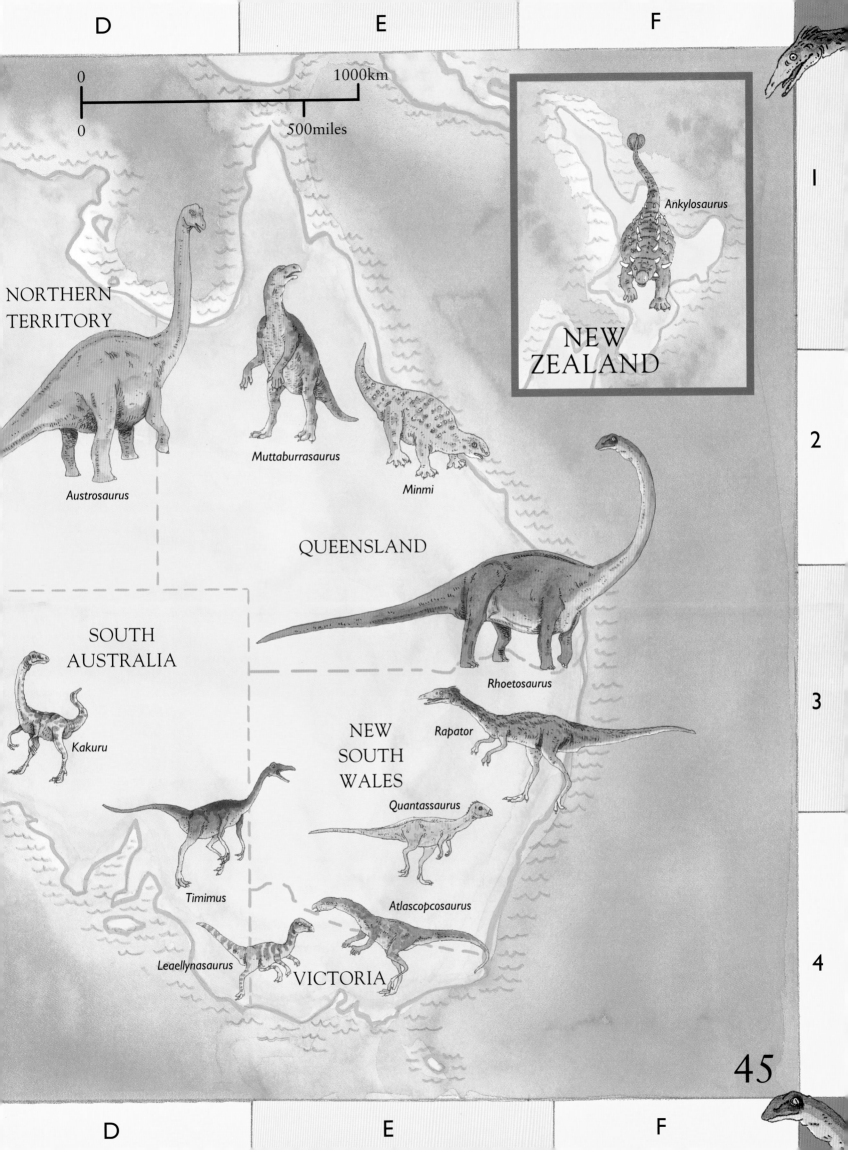

0   1000km

0   500miles

NORTHERN
TERRITORY

NEW
ZEALAND

Ankylosaurus

Austrosaurus

Muttaburrasaurus

Minmi

QUEENSLAND

SOUTH
AUSTRALIA

Rhoetosaurus

Kakuru

NEW
SOUTH
WALES

Rapator

Quantassaurus

Timimus

Atlascopcosaurus

Leaellynasaurus

VICTORIA

Glossary

ambush
To attack by surprise.

armoured dinosaur
A plant-eating dinosaur protected by tough scales or bony plates.

continent
One of Earth's seven huge blocks of land. In the age of the dinosaurs, the continents were in different positions than today.

crater
A deep hollow made by a volcano, or by a meteor hitting the Earth.

crest
A large flap on top of a dinosaur's head.

Cretaceous period
The last part of the age of the dinosaurs, which ended suddenly when a meteor struck the Earth.

dinosaur hunter
Someone who searches for dinosaur fossils and digs them out.

duck-bill dinosaur
A dinosaur with a mouth like a beak, and without front teeth. Also known as a hadrosaur.

evolve
Change gradually over thousands or millions of years. As living things evolve, new kinds gradually appear, while older ones slowly become extinct, or die out.

extinct
No longer living anywhere on Earth. The dinosaurs are now extinct, together with many other giant reptiles.

fossil
Hard parts of an animal's body that have been slowly changed to stone deep in the ground.

herd
A group of animals that live, feed and breed together.

horn
A hard body part with a sharp point, usually found on a dinosaur's head.

insect
A small animal with six legs, such as a beetle or a bee. The first insects appeared long before the first dinosaurs.

Jurassic period
The middle part of the age of the dinosaurs.

limb
A front or back leg.

limestone
A kind of layered rock that often contains fossils.

mammal
A warm-blooded animal that feeds its babies on milk.

meteor
A piece of rock that has reached the Earth from space.

naturalist
Someone who studies animals and plants.

nerves
Parts of the body that work like wiring, helping an animal to feel and to move.

Pangea
A huge supercontinent that existed at the beginning of the age of the dinosaurs.

predator
Any animal that hunts others for its food.

prehistoric
Anything that lived in the distant past, long before human history began.

prey
An animal that is hunted and eaten by another animal.

quarry
A place where rock is dug up so that it can be used. Quarries are often good places for finding fossils.

reptile
A cold-blooded animal with scaly skin, which usually breeds by laying eggs. Dinosaurs were the biggest reptiles that ever lived.

sauropod
A huge, long-necked dinosaur that fed on plants. The largest dinosaurs were all sauropods.

scales
Small, hard plates that cover a reptile's skin.

scavenging
Feeding on the remains of dead animals.

serrated
With jagged edges.

trackway
A place where dinosaurs often walked, leaving fossilized footprints.

Triassic period
The first part of the age of the dinosaurs.

Index

Each dinosaur name has a pronunciation guide in brackets after its entry.

Photographic acknowledgements

The Publisher would like to thank the following for permission to reproduce their material. Every care has been taken to trace copyright holders. However, if there have been unintentional omissions or failure to trace copyright holders, we apologise and will, if informed, endeavour to make corrections in any future edition.

Pages: 5 Natural History Museum, London; 9 Jonathan Blair/Corbis; 13 James L Amos/Corbis; 15 Natural History Museum, London; 19 D van Ravenswaay/Science photo Library; 20 Kevin Schafer/Corbis; 24 Sally A Morgan/Corbis; 26l Museum of Natural Science, Belgium; 26r Ian West; 29 Natural History Museum; 31 Didier Dutheil/Corbis; 33 DK Images; 35 University of Chicago; 37 Louie Psihoyos/Corbis; 39 Louie Psihoyos/Corbis; 41 Louie Psihoyos/Corbis; 44 CWB